Communiqué

Poems From The Headlines

Ed Werstein

Communiqué

Poems From The Headlines

Ed Werstein

Water's Edge Press

Copyright © 2021 by Ed Werstein

All rights reserved.

Printed in the United States of America

Water's Edge Press LLC
Sheboygan, WI
watersedgepress.com

ISBN: 978-1-952526-02-2
Library of Congress Control Number: 2021933239

Cover images licensed through VectorStock

A Water's Edge Press First Edition

For my grandchildren and all the world's children,
in hopes of a future worthy of them.

"If you would be a poet, write living newspapers. Be a reporter from outer space, filing dispatches to some supreme managing editor who believes in full disclosure and has a low tolerance for bullshit."

Lawrence Ferlinghetti, from *Poetry as Insurgent Art*

Facts Are Under Assault in 2020
  — Politifact website

Facts and Anti-Facts

The world is not a poem. –John Williams, from the novel, Augustus

Not a poem in the way a sunset is a poem
or a sunrise, or even in the way
a violent thunderstorm can
invade you like Yeats', *The Second Coming.*

No, lately the world is more like
a surreal documentary:
no room for poetry,
the news as science-fiction,
full of facts and anti-facts
and difficult to tell which is which.

But smash them together,
and they both disappear.

Contents

Facts and Anti-Facts

National and Local News

Coping Strategies 1
Runaway Balloon 2
Supporting the Troops 3
Transportation Blues 4
A Couple from Massachusetts 5
George Floyd at 100 Degrees Celsius 6
Dear Emmett 7
Monday Monday 8
A Pervert With Money 9
Another Useless Headline Poem 10

International News

Teaching Women How to Fly 13
Still Life 14
A Miner's Tide 15
On the Exhumation of the Body of Pablo Neruda 16
The (Evo) Moral(es) of the Story 17
The Empire Drones On 18

Weather Report

Junkman's Wet Dream 21
If Only 22
It's Not God, It's Us 23
Disappearing Icebergs 24
The Tepid Sea 25

Sports Report

Flag Football 29
All the Little Children Got 30
Change of Seasons 32
Ernie 33
Spring Hopes, Eternal 34
Gawker 35

Business News

Do Not Go Gentle Off That Overbooked Flight 39
It Takes a Treasury 40
Do Not Stare Directly 41
Mine 42
Austerity 43
Dying for Capitalism 44

Politics
Nothing From Zero Is Really Something 47
Fuck Alabama! 48
Second Thoughts 49
Horror Film 50
Lament For Dissent 51
Minute Sonnet 52
Inaugural Poem 53
Plutocracy 54

Special: The War Report
Karleton and Robert 57
May 4 58
The Ho Chi Minh Trail, Gulf of Tonkin, Weapons of
Mass Destruction, and Other Myth-information about Wars 59
Droning On 60
I'm Sorry 61
That Is Not Who We Are 62

Science and Religion
A Rapture Every Week 65
The Picture of Dorian Redwood 66
The Voices at Chauvet Cave 67
Telescope 68
Pan-Demonic 70
Two Millennia of Misogyny 72
Universe 73

Obituaries
On the Good Ship Lollipop 77
We All Lay Down 78
His Hammer 79
My Main Man Alex 80
The Smiling Mortician Foiled 81
Cicadas 82

1
National and Local News

Every day the news is a script like a cement truck of neoliberal terror already in progress.

Rejected ideals party bosses don't share. A violent thunderstorm can invade. It's never going to arrive.

We will be there in our thousands. He's not breathing, he's begging, and the gumption it might take to change things.

What is one life worth? Just hours before the earth shook. And now women are flying again, driven by junkyard vultures, gold, platinum, and palladium. They sang just for us.

Poetry will be shouted from rooftops and railway stops, days of hope and inspiration, just the stitching in the patchwork.

Innocent by anyone's standard, your red, white, and blue heart. It doesn't shine for you and these few words: austerity, crisis, foreclosure.

There's only one amendment.

We create because we must.

Eight out of 10 Women Have Felt Unable to Cope in the Past Year
— *The Guardian*, May 14, 2018

Coping Strategies

So, I'm wondering,
who are the other two?
What's their secret?
I'd like to learn
some of their coping strategies,
because, frankly, I'm not
coping too well myself.

Do they live on a deserted island?
Did they invest in a sensory deprivation tank?
Did one of them shoot Harvey Weinstein?
Set fire to a Trump Tower?
Was there alcohol involved?

If there was alcohol involved
I'd like to hear about it.

Feared Lost in Balloon, Boy Found at Home
— NBC News, April 4, 2010

Runaway Balloon

Sometimes we'd all be better
off in a box   in the attic
except for those times
when our
parents
put
us
there

Wisconsin Workers Protest Plan to Cut Benefits
— *New York Times*, February 16, 2011

Supporting the Troops

for the activists in the 2011 Wisconsin uprising

We support you, our heroes on the front line
we, who cannot be there daily,
who cannot brave the cold and snow,
who cannot spend the night on marble floors
protecting the rights of us all.
We will shovel your walks,
water your plants, feed your animals.

We will watch your children, read them stories
of your bravery and resolve, tell them
their parents are heroes, defending our freedoms.

We will post and re-post your messages,
your videos, your letters, your first-hand accounts,
your stories that don't make the corporate news.

We will feed you with pizza from down the street,
ordered for you from around the world.
We will write poetry and music in your honor.

And when we can
as soon as we can
every time that we can
we will be there in our thousands
reinforcing you, warming you
with our warm bodies and our love.

Wisconsin Governor Rejects $810 Million for High Speed Rail
— *In These Times,* November 16, 2010

Transportation Blues

"She caught the Katy and left me a mule to ride." –Taj Mahal

What will it mean to get untracked
or derailed when the trains are gone?

In the future, will unforeseen catastrophes
still be compared to getting hit by a train?

Will jilted lovers no longer be left standing
on the platform watching their mates board the Katy?

Will we all be left a mule to ride?
Will we ever get back on track?

How will we ease our troubled minds
when the 2:19 no longer comes by?

What clichés will we use
when all the trains are gone?

Note: The Katy was the popular name of the Missouri-Kansas-Texas Railway.

Hikers found dead after fall from icy cliff
at Acadia National Park, Maine
 — *Sacramento Bee*, March 21, 2021

A Couple from Massachusetts

were hiking in Maine, slipped on some ice
fell over 100 feet, and wound up dead.
My reaction to this news?

Irritation.

With news of war, mass shootings, a pandemic
and a looming environmental disaster,
Why do I need to know this?
An incident important to
no one but their relatives and neighbors.

On average 7,500 people die each day in the US.
Do I need to know about each one? But some of them,
like this couple from Massachusetts,
die in each others arms doing something they love to do.

I should be so lucky.

Week In Politics: Protests Erupt Nationwide
For Deaths Of George Floyd, Breonna Taylor
— *NPR*, May 30, 2020

George Floyd at 100 Degrees Celsius

"Quantitative changes suddenly become qualitative changes; differences in degree lead to differences in kind." –John Barth

It's water, it's water, it's water,
and suddenly,
it's steam. The pot boils.

Minneapolis:
George Floyd is alive,
he's breathing, he's breathing,
he's not breathing, he's begging,
he's not breathing, he's begging,
and 8 minutes and 46 seconds later,
he's dead. The country boils.

Louisville:
Breonna Taylor is alive,
and then not alive,
at least 20 rounds
fired by police,
at the wrong person,
in the wrong house.

Recent examples of frequent
abuse of police power
throughout US history.
The difference between
99 and 100 degrees.
The pot boiled.
The country boils.
The key is to keep it boiling.

Woman Linked to 1955 Emmett Till Murder
Tells Historian Her Claims Were False
 — *New York Times*, January 27, 2017

Dear Emmett

You're dead, your mother is dead, Roy Bryant and J. W. Milam,
the men who murdered you and were acquitted, are dead.

The investigation was officially closed long ago. "Bow thy head
O state of Mississippi, Let tears of shame course down thy cheek,"

wrote Langston Hughes at that time. And there is still so much hate
in Mississippi. They had to re-make your memorial in 2019.
It's bulletproof now.

Emmett, only the woman, Carolyn Bryant Donham, who accused you
of ogling and whistling, is still alive. Now, with death approaching,

she wants to recant her testimony, to unburden her troubled soul.
I wish she had a soul. I wish there were a
hell for that soul to suffer in.

Your hell, Emmett, was here on Earth. Is justice
60 years late any justice at all?
Emmett, you're still gone. Is America any
different than on the day you died?

Las Vegas Shooting: 58 Killed, Almost 500 Injured
— NBC News, October 2, 2017

Monday Monday

This is the Mondayest of Mondays
like the first Monday of a new school year
like the Monday after the World Series
a binge-weekend's Monday hangover
the first dark Monday after the fall time change
the first Monday of a prison sentence
the Monday after you bury your mother.
This is the mother of all Mondays.

This is the eleven thousand nine hundred and sixty first
consecutive Monday that the US Constitution
has failed to provide health care to all.

This is the one thousand nine hundred and thirteenth
consecutive Monday that more American tax dollars
have been given to the rich than to the poor.

This is the three thousand seven hundred ninety sixth
consecutive Monday without a U.S. ban on assault weapons.
This is the Mondayest of all Mondays.

Rudy Giuliani caught in compromising position in new 'Borat' film
— NBC News, October 21, 2020

A Pervert With Money

"how my flesh summers" –Eavan Boland

She masturbates.
I watch.

I'm not ashamed.
I paid for this.

She doesn't have to touch
anything but herself.

I know she's pretending.
I don't care.

Good acting costs money.
I unzip.

Orlando Gunman Attacks Gay Nightclub, Leaving 50 Dead
— *New York Times*, June 16, 2016

Another Useless Headline Poem

I've been thinking about flesh
and blood
and guts
and guns
and bullets
and assaults
on our sanity.

And I've been thinking about guts
and guns
and gold
and gilt
and guilt
and gullibility
and gushing blood
and the gumption
it might take
to change things.

And I've been thinking about how
we must not be
disgruntled enough
disgusted enough
about how we must not be
dis-gutted enough
to stop watching the news reports
to stop posting on Facebook
to stop writing ineffective
and useless poems
about it
to finally rise up
and do something real
to change it.

2
International News

Every day the news is a script like a cement truck of neoliberal terror already in progress.

Rejected ideals party bosses don't share. A violent thunderstorm can invade. It's never going to arrive.

We will be there in our thousands. He's not breathing, he's begging, and the gumption it might take to change things.

What is one life worth? Just hours before the earth shook. And now women are flying again, driven by junkyard vultures, gold, platinum, and palladium. they sang just for us.

Poetry will be shouted from rooftops and railway stops, days of hope and inspiration, just the stitching in the patchwork.

Innocent by anyone's standard, your red, white, and blue heart. It doesn't shine for you and these few words: austerity, crisis, foreclosure.

There's only one amendment.

We create because we must.

A Somber Centennial for the Triangle Factory Fire
— *NPR*, March 24, 2011

Teaching Women How to Fly

On December 14, 2010, more than 30 workers died and 100 were injured when they jumped from upper floor windows to escape a garment factory fire in Dhaka, Bangladesh.

Your great-grandparents marched
for safety, "Bread and Roses!"
after the fire forced the women to jump
from windows at the Triangle Shirtwaist factory
in New York City in 1911.

Your grandparents fought and died
for safety, "Bread and Roses!"
at Flint in 1937.
Held the GM factory for weeks
to win their union.

Your parents picketed
time and again
for safety, "Bread and Roses!"
to protect their unions
in what has become the Rust Belt.

And now women are flying again
falling from factory windows in Bangladesh
while you wait in line at Walmart
to buy the shirts they were sewing
on the day before they died,
died to make the owners richer.

Owners whose ancestors owned
shirt factories in New York.
Owners who now are looking
for other women,
in even poorer countries,
to teach them how to fly.

Deadly Earthquake Hits Central Chile
  — *The Guardian*, February 27, 2010

Still Life

In the photos taken just hours before
the earth shook, you are smiling,
happy to have a Wisconsin visitor,
happy to talk baseball and American politics.
Happy to introduce someone new
to the flavors of pastel de choclo,
that most authentic of Chilean cuisine,
which sits cooling in front of you,
its thick, sweet corn crust,
like the crust of Chile, still unbroken,
but bubbling beneath its surface.

Later, after the meal and the Malbec,
our friend, your visitor, walks to his hotel,
and you, your wife, and my grandson
board the Metro heading for home,
all of you still smiling, still unaware
of the earth's deeper motion,
unaware of the trembling night ahead.

Unaware that just off the coast,
frantic fish are already heading
for deeper waters.

All 33 Trapped Chilean Miners Have Been Rescued After 69 Days
— *The Guardian*, October 13, 2010

A Miner's Tide

We've lost something here;
it would be good to get it back.
There's too much polarity
in the northern hemisphere.
Here we dig trenches of isolation:
What color is your state?
let the poor starve
let the weak wither
let the homeless freeze.

We paint our lost sheep
colors other than human.

South of the equator
they dig tunnels of salvation
for a few lost sheep
swallowed by the earth.

There, in Chile,
where you are never too far
from the sea, they know
that all boats rise with the tide.

And now, the spirit of the world
has risen with the miners of Copiapó, Chile!

Chilean Poet Pablo Neruda's Body to Be Exhumed
— *BBC News*, February 9, 2013

On the Exhumation of the Body of Pablo Neruda

Isla Negra, Chile, April 8, 2013

Dear Pablo,

The whole world knows who and what killed you.
Bringing up your body is just a media show.

Would the discovery of arsenic or cyanide
make the guilty any more guilty? Poison or no poison,
your spirit was crushed along with Chile's democracy.
But the government had to come up with some excuse
for examining your body. And now that the old dictator
is dead, they can afford to lay another rap on his record.

After all, like I said, would 3,001 deaths make Pinochet
more culpable than 3,000? No, they aren't looking
for poison. The real reason for the exhumation is that
the junta wasn't able to kill your poetry. People think you may
have been buried alive. They're searching for the beating heart
of your poetry. But they won't find it there in your grave.
The heart of your poetry beats on around the world.

The Coup That Ousted Evo Morales
— *CounterPunch*, November 20, 2019

The (Evo) Moral(es) of the Story

And democracy disappeared
with the icebergs
in the great magic act
of capitalism.

Biden said 'Diplomacy is back!' Then he started dropping bombs
 — *The Guardian*, February 26, 2021

The Empire Drones On

This is our punishment
for always choosing the lesser of two evils.

To celebrate the return (the continuation)
of the American assault on the rest of the world.

Once again America has refused to join
with what's left of the enlightened human race.

Once again we refuse to take a seat at the table
of sanity. The world is running out of patience.

The world is running out of time.
The empire drones on despite its death throes.

We will be punished for this. And when we are,
we will see the headlines of surprise again.

No one could have seen this coming.
Wise up, America, although it's already too late.

Everybody can see it coming but you.

3
Weather Report

Every day the news is a script like a cement truck of neoliberal terror already in progress.

Rejected ideals party bosses don't share. A violent thunderstorm can invade. It's never going to arrive.

We will be there in our thousands. He's not breathing, he's begging, and the gumption it might take to change things.

What is one life worth? Just hours before the earth shook. And now women are flying again, driven by junkyard vultures, gold, platinum, and palladium. they sang just for us.

Poetry will be shouted from rooftops and railway stops, days of hope and inspiration, just the stitching in the patchwork.

Innocent by anyone's standard, your red, white, and blue heart. It doesn't shine for you and these few words: austerity, crisis, foreclosure.

There's only one amendment.

We create because we must.

Storms Leave 160 Basements Damaged
— *Milwaukee Journal Sentinel*, July 17, 2010

Junkman's Wet Dream

Even if the old stories are true,
God hasn't spoken up in a very long time.
Maybe he doesn't care
if anyone survives the next flood.

Meteorologists aren't quite as accurate
at forecasting big rains. So people tend
to ignore them. It's hard to ignore a bush
bursting into flames, a blinding light
that unsaddles you, a Robeson-like voice
that rumbles, Noah, listen!

The local weathermen, sandwiched
between commercials for Arby's
and Subway, just don't have as much thunder.

But this time they got it right,
those prognosticators of precipitation,
and the rains came. Sewers slowed
and basements filled.

Today, in the sunshine, people all over the city
are hauling water-soaked hutches, cabinets
and carpets to the curb as old pickup trucks,
driven by junkyard vultures, circle
like Conestogas making camp,
like planes over La Guardia,
like toms around a cat in heat,
ready to pounce.

Fog Forces Cancellation of Milwaukee Air Show
— *Milwaukee Journal-Sentinel*, June 21, 2014

If Only

If only it were that easy to stop a real bombing raid
mothers all over the world would pray for bad weather
every day, to spare their homes, their homelands
their children.

But here on Milwaukee's lakefront
the spectacle is rescheduled for tomorrow.

This roaring assault on eardrums and sensibilities
is nothing compared to the price paid by others
for the live-ammo show, rain or shine.

Here, parents bring the kids, wave flags
eat ice cream.

Kirk Cameron: God Sends Hurricanes to Teach Us Repentance
— *The Daily Beast,* September 8, 2017

It's Not God, It's Us

We're on our own here, killing each other
and killing Mother Earth.

From persistent drought:
dust you are, and to dust you shall return
to relentless hurricanes:
from the swamp you came, and there you shall return.

One hundred-year storms, droughts, and fires
compete daily for news coverage, but still
some say climate change is a hoax.

Wrong. Human intelligence is a hoax.
We've been mesmerized, paralyzed by the spectacle
in its many costumes: religion, football, television,
gambling, drugs, alcohol, none of which are evil,
in moderation. Well OK, football; but they are all
versions of the spectacle that shields us from the truth.

Instantaneous news feeds allow us to watch 24/7
as our fellow human beings cope with hurricanes
or floods. And after things settle for them,
they get their TV working just in time
to watch others flee a forest fire or tsunami.
Later, both watch as an iceberg the size of Delaware
drops into the North Atlantic. But don't protest
or take any action, except maybe sending a few bucks:
our only way to make up for a strangled government.

Don't demonstrate, and if you must chant, just keep chanting,
Go Pack Go! and Climate Change is a Hoax!

Greta Thunberg Gives Powerful Speech at UN Climate Summit
— *Time*, September 23, 2019

Disappearing Icebergs

Things tend to happen
after you stop worrying
about them. Like when
two hours after you've
flossed and brushed
then flossed again
the popcorn hull just drops
from between two molars
onto your tongue.

Or the way your lost
tortoiseshell shoehorn
plops from under the tongue
of your dress shoes
the next time you wear them.

Or the way just when
you've finally given up
on humanity and accepted
disappearing icebergs
and climate catastrophe,
Greta Thunberg
stops in at the U.N.
to give them a tongue-
lashing.

Climate emergency: world 'may have crossed tipping point'
 — *The Guardian*, November 27, 2019

The Tepid Sea

At the end of the world poetry will be shouted
from rooftops and railway stops
from beaches and balconies
from church steeples and the minarets of mosques.

At the end of the world poetry will be screamed
from soapboxes on street corners
from a burning rain forest
from the rocky moraine of a vanishing glacier.

At the last poetry reading at the end of the world
the last poets will speak from the ice
of the last berg melting into the warming water.

As each poet recites their farewell poem,
they will slip into the salty tea of that tepid sea.

And as the final poet recites the final poem
at the end of the world (appropriately, an elegy
or a lament, but not an epic, as time will be short),
as this last poet does, for the last time, what poets
have always done, there will be no one left to listen.

4
Sports Report

Every day the news is a script like a cement truck of neoliberal terror already in progress.

Rejected ideals party bosses don't share. A violent thunderstorm can invade. It's never going to arrive.

We will be there in our thousands. He's not breathing, he's begging, and the gumption it might take to change things.

What is one life worth? Just hours before the earth shook. And now women are flying again, driven by junkyard vultures, gold, platinum, and palladium. they sang just for us.

Poetry will be shouted from rooftops and railway stops, days of hope and inspiration, just the stitching in the patchwork.

Innocent by anyone's standard, your red, white, and blue heart. It doesn't shine for you and these few words: austerity, crisis, foreclosure.

There's only one amendment.

We create because we must.

Trump Blasts NFL Players for Kneeling During Anthem
 — ABC News, August 10, 2018

Flag Football

The president tweeted his little whistle
and threw the flag in front of the protesting players.
For once the players weren't trying to call attention
to themselves. For once they weren't stomping
or goose-stepping around the field beating their chests
with their "I'm number one" finger pointing
toward the heavens, or jumping into the laps
of joyous fans. They were kneeling.

Simply kneeling, to call attention to an injustice
suffered by others, and to call attention to the fact
that they saw this as an American problem.

The problem for the president was they weren't kneeling to him.
So he tweeted his whistle as referee-in-chief
and threw the flag. The call was unpatriotic conduct.

The president wanted the NFL renamed The National Flag League.
He wanted the ball replaced and a flag marched
up and down the field instead

in an even more war-like game to match the militaristic fever
he wanted to stir up in the country.
Most of all, he wanted the players penalized.
He was used to people kneeling,
but right in front of him,
and for a different reason.

Concussions, Broken Bones, and More: a Week of Football in the US
— *StatNews*, November, 2019

All the Little Children Got

for my grandsons Anthony, Oliver, and Matías

Derek Newton, Houston Texans, elbow.
Anthony's got an elbow
Ollie's got an elbow
Matí's got an elbow
all the little children got

Jeff Heath, Dallas Cowboys, shoulder.
Anthony's got a shoulder
Ollie's got a shoulder
Matí's got a shoulder
all the little children got

Pernell McPhee, Chicago Bears, knee.
Anthony's got a knee
Ollie's got a knee
Matí's got a knee
all the little children got

Dannell Ellerbe, New Orleans Saints, hip.
Anthony's got a hip
Ollie's got a hip
Matí's got a hip
all the little children got

Matt Hasselbeck, Indianapolis Colts, back.
Anthony's got a back
Ollie's got a back
Matí's got a back
all the little children got

Sam Shields, Green Bay Packers, concussion.
Anthony's got a brain
Ollie's got a brain
Matí's got a brain
all the little children got...

Aaron Rodgers Breaks Collarbone, Could Miss Season
 — ESPN, October 15, 2017

Change of Seasons

Oh My God! Our quarterback is down!
Look! They're escorting him off the field.
It might be a broken collar bone.

All our cheering now turned to silent frowns.
Where has this replacement been concealed?
Good Lord! Our quarterback is down!

This sure win will surely now be blown.
And against these Vikings! Such a rotten deal!
It could be a broken collar bone.

It's such a pain each time we lose to these clowns.
Now our victory is theirs to steal.
Lord help us! Our quarterback is down!

Simultaneously all bookmakers reach for their phones,
asking what the X-rays have revealed.
A fractured clavicle? That's the collar bone!

Oh, why couldn't the back-up be a clone?
Brett Hundley?? How long till Aaron Rodgers heals?
Aaron Rodgers has broken his collarbone.
Sweet Jesus, no! Our quarterback is down!

Ernie Harwell, Longtime Tiger Broadcaster, Dies at 92
— *New York Times*, May 4, 2010

Ernie

Five minutes after tuning in late, you knew all the important stuff:
the score, inning, situation, pitchers, key plays, game summary,

the Tiges (Ernie often called them "Tiges")
scored first on Kaline's sacrifice fly in the third,
but the Bosox took the lead in their half of the inning
with a two-run blast by Malzone after a one-out walk to Runnels.

If the Tigers were on the road, you got additional information.
Maybe a description of Chicago's Comiskey Park
with those beautiful arches, or the dimensions
of the green monster at Boston's Fenway Park.

But the stats were just the stitching in the patchwork
of beautiful pictures he pieced together.

Moms from Midland, that lad from Lansing,
and the gentleman from Ypsilanti
will still manage to snag foul balls.

Hitters will still just stand there, watching called third strikes
sail by *like the proverbial house by the side of the road.*

Double plays will still be *two for the price of one*,
homers will still be *lo...o...ong gone*, and fans will still be
holding on to their Strohs during those tense ninth innings.

But, like a ground-rule double he's *hopped the fence*
and left the park. Ernie Harwell is gone,
and no one will ever tell us that way again.

Brewers pitchers and catchers take part
in first official workout of 2020
   — *Milwaukee Journal-Sentinel*, February 16, 2020

Spring Hopes, Eternal

I'd like to report the report
of a fastball rifled into a catcher's mitt
for the first time since October.

Before songbirds return north,
before the calendar turns to fickle March,
before Wisconsin weather turns,

spring hopes, eternal hopes, return.
Pitchers and catchers report. It will snow
again soon, and iced mornings

may persist here in the north,
but winter's worst woe has been weathered
The silence has been broken.

Brewers found a unique way to advance to the
playoffs for the third consecutive season
  — *Milwaukee Journal-Sentinel*, September 27, 2020

Gawker

In this season of no stadium traffic there are still accidents.

For instance, your team accidentally backed into the playoffs
like a cement truck without a reverse beeper.

In this season where over half the teams collided into the playoffs,
six more than last year, your team is the sixteenth one in.

The last one. Like the playground dweeb who gets to play
because somebody has to play right field, they limped in.

In this wreck of a season, your team had to
hobble out to the west coast,
where games start two hours later than local time. You don't want
to stay up late, but hey, it's an accident.

You just can't help but gawk.

5
Business News

Every day the news is a script like a cement truck of neoliberal terror already in progress.

Rejected ideals party bosses don't share. A violent thunderstorm can invade. It's never going to arrive.

We will be there in our thousands. He's not breathing, he's begging, and the gumption it might take to change things.

What is one life worth? Just hours before the earth shook. And now women are flying again, driven by junkyard vultures, gold, platinum, and palladium. they sang just for us.

Poetry will be shouted from rooftops and railway stops, days of hope and inspiration, just the stitching in the patchwork.

Innocent by anyone's standard, your red, white, and blue heart. It doesn't shine for you and these few words: austerity, crisis, foreclosure.

There's only one amendment.

We create because we must.

Passenger Dragged Off Overbooked United Flight
— CNN, April 10, 2018

Do Not Go Gentle Off That Overbooked Flight

after Dylan Thomas

Do not go gentle off that overbooked flight;
You've a ticket just like the others! Dig in, stay.
Rage, rage and put up a good fight.

An algorithm doesn't make it fair or right,
No matter what United's policies say.
Do not go gentle off that overbooked flight.

The friendly skies aren't looking so bright;
Facebook and YouTube show us the way
He raged, raged and put up a good fight.

I'm telling you right now, they could just bite
Me. If that happened to me one day,
I'd not go gentle off that overbooked flight.

The CEOs, grave men, must be turning white.
I hope he sues them and makes them pay.
Rage, rage and put up a legal fight.

And you, traveler, searching Priceline or some such site
For tickets to some place far, far away,
Do not go gentle off that overbooked flight.
Rage, rage, and put up a good fight.

Hamilton Ticket Scalpers Pocket $240,000 Per Week
— *Bloomberg Market Report,* May, 2016

It Takes a Treasury

Ticket prices are approaching $2,000 each.
How ironic. Hamilton was our nation's first Secretary
of the Treasury, our country's first banker.

And now it takes 200 Hamiltons
to purchase one ticket to see the show.

Stock Market Closing in on All-time High
  — CNBC News, June 11, 2019

Do Not Stare Directly

Do not stare directly into Wall Street's blinding light
as the Dow Jones approaches an all-time high.
It doesn't glow for you, but for those you need to fight.

Though tempted at times in the quiet of the night
to get out your laptop and search for stocks to buy,
that urge comes from staring at Wall Street's blinding light.

It's growing credit-spending that makes its glow so bright.
Your bills arrive, the bankers smile, and you begin to cry.
Their light shines not for you, but for those you need to fight.

The middle class is shrinking and you think you'll never quite
get out from under all those mounting debts before you die.
You must not stare directly into Wall Street's blinding light.

Fewer jobs and lower pay is the modern worker's plight.
At intersections, homeless folks beg as you pass by.
The Dow shines not on you, but on those you need to fight.

Defy their corporate greed and austerity plans. You might
even learn the economic reasons why
you mustn't stare directly into Wall Street's glowing light.
It doesn't shine for you but for those you need to fight.

Protesters Interrupt Drilling in Penokees
 — Wisconsin Public Radio, June 12, 2013

Mine

I say, it's mine. You know who I am.
Mine is mine, and those things
you thought were yours? They're mine.

The mines are mine. All the mines
that miners mined and died in
or out of. They're mine.
And that mine that is not a mine yet?
That mine you don't want?
It will be a mine, and it will be mine.

Protest and speak out all you want,
I've got my people working on it.
They're mining the constitution.

You didn't think that was yours, did you?

I'll sing you part of an old refrain:
This land is MY land... I forget the rest.

The oil is mine, the water, mine,
even the wind. I'll meter it and sell it to you
as soon as you buy all my oil.

Yes, the earth is mine! And when I'm gone
it's going to stay in the family—inherited.

And don't give me any of that
the meek will inherit the earth crap.
You wanna get yourself crucified?

UN Calls for Economic Makeover to Replace Neo-liberalism
 — *Business News*, September, 2017

Austerity

*The text of this poem has been appropriated as a payment of debts owed.**

*Note:
What if, like other states, the state of poetry were in default?
Poets everywhere would be in debt.
A word lifted here, a phrase there,
a borrowed reference
and pretty soon it would start to add up.

The lenders, wildly rich
with words piled high in library vaults
(words like money, gold, jewelry,
estates, offshore bank accounts,
portfolios and Porsches),
would lend to us
at ever-increasing interest rates.

We would continue to write,
but eventually our words would
disappear as we wrote them,
repossessed.

We would be left with only titles,
signifying not our ownership
but our mounting debts,
and these few words: austerity,
crisis, foreclosure, unemployment,
hunger, poverty, war.

Words that would never be taken from us.

Trump's Death Cult Finally Says It: Time to Kill
the "Useless Eaters" for Capitalism
— *Salon*, March 27, 2020

Dying for Capitalism

Not as in, I miss you and I'm dying
to see you again soon. Which is something
I've said to my grandchildren each day
since their school closed in this pandemic.

My children don't want me to visit
because they love me, and because
I'm among the aging and vulnerable.
Trump's death cult means it literally,
dying for capitalism.

"Useless eaters," they call us, the retired
and unemployed. In the view of the elites,
loyalty to country should lead the elderly
to sacrifice what's left of their short lives
for the sake of the economy.

Capitalism has been killing us,
literally,
for hundreds of years. I'm thinking,
it's about time capitalism died for us.

6
Politics

Every day the news is a script like a cement truck of neoliberal terror already in progress.

Rejected ideals party bosses don't share. A violent thunderstorm can invade. It's never going to arrive.

We will be there in our thousands. He's not breathing, he's begging, and the gumption it might take to change things.

What is one life worth? Just hours before the earth shook. And now women are flying again, driven by junkyard vultures, gold, platinum, and palladium. they sang just for us.

Poetry will be shouted from rooftops and railway stops, days of hope and inspiration, just the stitching in the patchwork.

Innocent by anyone's standard, your red, white, and blue heart. It doesn't shine for you and these few words: austerity, crisis, foreclosure.

There's only one amendment.

We create because we must.

Zero Mostel Testifies Before HUAC
  — *Alpha History*, August 10, 1955

Nothing From Zero Is Really Something

When put to the test
You were one of the best
You didn't play games
You didn't name names
Zero our hero
You're the Most(el).

Alabama Senate Passes Bill Banning Nearly All Abortion
— FOX News, May 14, 2019

Fuck Alabama!

I wish I were living in a country that had allowed
the Southern States to secede. No shots fired save
the opening salvo at Sumter. Then, *Oh!*
You want to leave? OK then. It's all yours.

I wish I were living in a country that had withdrawn
from the South and then drawn a firm border, built
a wall even. *Everyone has six weeks to get in*
or get out. Make up your mind! Then slammed the door.

I wish I were living in a country that had then infiltrated
the Confederacy, sending spies on missions to free slaves
and help them North to freedom. And then refused
any request for extradition. *Pick your own damn cotton!*

I wish I were living in a country where George Wallace,
Lester Maddox, Jesse Helms, Jeff Sessions,
Stonewall Jackson, and Jefferson Davis
were historical figures in somebody else's country.

I wish I were living in a country that had then abolished
all remaining state borders. One country that welcomed all.
The promise of an American republic that allowed everyone
to vote, and then declared the person with the most votes
the winner. Fuck Alabama!

Virginia Legislature Turns Down Ban on Military-style Weapons
 — *New York Times*, February 17, 2020

Second Thoughts

Above all else on Earth I love my guns.
They're symbols of my freedom and my rights.
Each and every citizen should own one.

The deadliest of arms for sale beneath the sun
can put me on the top in any fight.
Above all else on Earth I love my guns.

The founding fathers would scratch their heads and wonder why liberal dweebs can't seem to see the light.
Each and every citizen should own one.

On second thought, not each and every one.
Just each and every citizen who's white.
Above all else on Earth I love my guns.

Above my wife, my daughters and my sons
whose lives my guns protect throughout the night.
Each and every citizen should own one.

Opposing points of view I always shun.
There's only one amendment I can cite.
Each and every citizen should own one.
Above all else on Earth I love my guns.

Rush Limbaugh Awarded Medal of Freedom
  — CNN, February 4, 2020

Horror Film

It's these times, or a depression
caused by these times, dystopia
no longer reserved for fiction.

What can one write when reality is stranger
than fiction, when every day the news is a script
from a horror film, every news item
building suspense toward the protagonist's doom?

Only it's one's entire species that is the doomed protagonist.
Who is directing this spectacle anyway?

Are we all just bit players in a cast of billions,
lorded over by over-paid stars?

Could we yet write a role for ourselves
that could turn this tragedy into an heroic epic
wherein the monster is vanquished, the asteroid avoided,
the bomb doesn't explode, the demonic villain is done in?
And in which, afterward, the bit players
form their own company, a cooperative,
that launches a world tour spreading the good news.

Trump Inauguration Protesters Go on Trial
 — *USA Today*, November 20, 2017

Lament For Dissent

Now is the winter of our discounted dissent,
the winter when we do not look forward to spring
and the melting glaciers, the rising waters
threatening Liberty's torch there in the harbor.
Will she abandon her pedestal in disgust,
beacon blown out by hurricane gusts,
tears in her eyes from the smoke of a thousand fires?

Liberty's armor of reason is no match for treason's
lies and denials, its full arsenal of weaponry,
its super-sized ammo magazines,
a lunatic's finger on the button to oblivion.

AOC Only Gets 60 Seconds At Democratic Convention To Deliver Pre-Recorded Message
— *Forbes Magazine*, August 12, 2020

Minute Sonnet

Minute woman
modern Minuteman
recording a minute waltz
for the diminished convention.

Only a spare minute
for the failed planks
and rejected ideals
party bosses don't share.

If she goes over the limit
cut off in a New York minute
steamed like Minute Rice
while we, the people, pay the price,

coerced into another seedy choice.
The chances for party reform: very minute.

The Irish For Hope and History Rhyme - What Will Biden's Inaugural Poem Be?
— *TheJournal.ie*, December, 2020

Inaugural Poem

We now return you to our
regularly scheduled programming
of neo-liberal terror,
already in progress.

Money Unlimited: The Citizens United Decision
— *The New Yorker*, May 21, 2012

Plutocracy

We are people too,
not ordinary folk, of course,
but supermen,
supreme in every way.

Knighted by courts,
judged able to speak freely,
with voices as loud
as our corporate bank accounts.

We speak with all the opinions
and votes our money can buy.
Truth bows when we speak our power.

Special: The War Report

Every day the news is a script like a cement truck of neoliberal terror already in progress.

Rejected ideals party bosses don't share. A violent thunderstorm can invade. It's never going to arrive.

We will be there in our thousands. He's not breathing, he's begging, and the gumption it might take to change things.

What is one life worth? Just hours before the earth shook. And now women are flying again, driven by junkyard vultures, gold, platinum, and palladium. they sang just for us.

Poetry will be shouted from rooftops and railway stops, days of hope and inspiration, just the stitching in the patchwork.

Innocent by anyone's standard, your red, white, and blue heart. It doesn't shine for you and these few words: austerity, crisis, foreclosure.

There's only one amendment.

We create because we must.

Bomb Blast at UW Kills One, Injures Four
— *Wisconsin State Journal*, August 25, 1970

Karleton and Robert

Karleton Armstrong wanted to fly,
wanted to bring the war home
by dropping bombs from the air, the way
U.S. soldiers were dropping them
on the Vietnamese. He wanted to re-create
in a small way what was going on over there.
But the bombs he dropped on the Badger
Army Ammunition plant failed to detonate.

Plan B was to blow up the Army Math Research Center
in Sterling Hall on the UW Madison campus.
Parts of the van/bomb he used were found
atop an eight-story building three blocks away.

Then in the morning news: Robert Fassnacht
had been working late. He was killed in the explosion.
Robert Fassnacht had a face, a family.
But so did the 1.1 million Asian victims
of napalm, land mines and carpet bombing
carried out by American pilots.
U.S. soldiers never knew the names of those they killed.
Many didn't even consider them human.
It was part of the training, the conditioning.
Did their anonymity make those lives less valuable?
Did Karleton consider Robert's death collateral damage?

What is one life worth?
What are a million?

"My God! They're Killing Us"
— *Newsweek*, May, 1970

May 4

Maybe William Knox Schroeder thought that joining ROTC was his way out of the ridiculous war going on in Southeast Asia, or maybe he couldn't wait to graduate and volunteer for overseas duty. We can't know. He can't tell us because he never graduated. One thing we do know is that he was not protesting that war when he was killed. He and Sandra Scheuer were walking between classes on May 4, 1970, on the Kent State University campus when the Ohio National Guard opened fire, killing them both, and two others who were protesting the war (was that a capital offense?), Allison Krause and Jeffrey Miller. Would it seem strange to you if I were to say that Allison and Jeffrey died protecting our freedom? Weren't they doing more to protect our freedom than the thousands of working-class kids conscripted and killed not knowing what in that hell they were fighting for? Maybe not. I don't know. I do know it's a matter of chance that they were killed and not me, protesting here in Wisconsin. And that's part of why I want to remember them, as feeble as the gesture may be. I wish I could do more. I wish I could tell you the names of the thousands of innocent Cambodians killed in the invasion that was being protested. I wish I could tell you the names of the thousands of innocent Vietnamese killed, disfigured by napalm rain, born disfigured, or maimed since by landmines in the rice paddies. But I can't. So for today, this anniversary, let these four names so inadequately represent all of them, all those dead and all the dead in all the pointless war since:

William Schroeder, Sandra Scheuer, Allison Krause, Jeffrey Miller.

US BOMBING N. VIET PORTS
 —*Los Angeles Times*, August 5, 1964

The Ho Chi Minh Trail, Gulf of Tonkin, Weapons of Mass Destruction, and Other Myth-information about Wars

The U.S.A. is bringing democracy to the world. It's
an easy sell (if you believe it), believe me!
And such a deal for us. We impose democracy (what we call
democracy) in exchange for natural resources and access to your
markets. With gold, platinum, and palladium we build smart phones,
or, rather, have you build them for us. With these
precious metals, plus titanium, we build bombers,
then drop bombs on the next country we manifest
against. Those bombers don't fly on democracy,
you know. We need your oil!

On the Ho Chi Minh Trail
footsteps
the shape of a country.

2,714 People Killed in 409 US Drone Attacks
in Pakistan Since January 2004
  — *The Economic Times,* November 9, 2018

Droning On

You don't want me to tell you about drones
but I'm going to tell you anyway.

You don't want to think about drones
killing innocent people in Pakistan
drones that you paid for, that we paid for.

Innocent people that thought things would be better
with a different US President. Instead they are worse,
yes, I said worse, especially if you are a dead Pakistani.

And yes, I know you don't want me to tell you about it,
that a president you helped elect, that you celebrated
and cried over, that our first Black president is a war criminal.

But I'm telling you, and it's true. You don't want to think
about your tax dollars, our tax dollars, killing innocent people.
Innocent by anyone's standard, as innocent as your grandchild.

You don't want me to tell you, and I don't want to have to
tell you, but I don't want to think about it alone.
I want you to tell me, what are we going to do?

US Hostage Kayla Mueller Killed by ISIS
  — *BBC News, September 10, 2015*

I'm Sorry

Do not mourn for Kayla
unless you truly grasp what killed her.

Do not mourn unless you are willing to mourn
every innocent child blown to bits
by American shock and awe. Unless you are willing
to cry for the lie of smart bombs and drones.

Do not sympathize with the pain and loss
of Kayla's mother unless you are willing to grasp

every mourning mother in the world,
pull her close to you and hold her tight,

letting her tears flow, wetting your red, white,
and blue heart, as you whisper over and over into her ear:

I'm sorry, I'm sorry.

Staff Sgt. Robert Bales Faces Murder Charges in Afghan Killings
— *New York Times*, March 24, 2012

That Is Not Who We Are

"That is not who we are." –Hillary Clinton, Secretary of State

Sixteen civilians shot dead in Kandahar
a soldier snaps and sixteen die,
mostly women and children.
A soldier snaps: three tours of duty in Iraq,
now deployed in Afghanistan.
He snaps, sixteen dead.
And Hillary says, that is not who we are.
Well, who are we then?

Are we the Marines who unzipped
and pissed on their victims?
Are we the soldiers who burned the Quran?

Are we Navy Seals who steal across borders
in midnight invasions to assassinate their prey
and anyone else who gets in the way?

Are we predator drones piloted by bunkered
joystick jockeys, raining terror on the guilty
and innocent alike? They see their kids each night
and never snap thinking about the ones they've killed.

Are we people who fight terror with terror,
who send young parents on continuous deployment
to unending wars against undefined enemies
and then act surprised when one of them snaps?

We didn't foresee that happening.
No one could have seen that coming.
Nobody except anybody
that is not who we are.

8
Science and Religion

Every day the news is a script like a cement truck of neoliberal terror already in progress.

Rejected ideals party bosses don't share. A violent thunderstorm can invade. It's never going to arrive.

We will be there in our thousands. He's not breathing, he's begging, and the gumption it might take to change things.

What is one life worth? Just hours before the earth shook. And now women are flying again, driven by junkyard vultures, gold, platinum, and palladium. they sang just for us.

Poetry will be shouted from rooftops and railway stops, days of hope and inspiration, just the stitching in the patchwork.

Innocent by anyone's standard, your red, white, and blue heart. It doesn't shine for you and these few words: austerity, crisis, foreclosure.

There's only one amendment.

We create because we must.

Rapture 2011: Is May 21st End of the World?
— ABC News, May 20, 2011

A Rapture Every Week

> "Over 22,000 children around the world die every day." –Global Issues website, 2011

You're still here. No rapture yesterday.
I'm sorry, I really am. But here you are, so
what are you going to do about it?

Go back to The Book? Recalculate? Rework
the hidden code, the secret set of equations
that will deliver you straight into the arms of Jesus?

Maybe yesterday he was busy with the children
that made it to Heaven without you. 22,000 children
died yesterday. Every day. A rapture of kids every week.

I'm not a believer, but if you are, you must believe
they went straight to Jesus, those innocents
with their scrawny fingers pawing their mothers'

dry breasts, wondering. Or drowned in floods,
crushed in earthquakes, war dead euphemized
as collateral damage. Instead of reworking

those calculations, why not polish your souls a bit,
oh, chosen ones? Couldn't you try to make the earth
a better place while you're waiting here for Jesus to return?

Even I could believe in that.

Redwoods: The Super Trees
—*National Geographic*, October 2009

The Picture of Dorian Redwood

> *"Forestry researchers have discovered that redwood trees produce denser, harder wood, and more of it, as they grow, to the age of about 1500 years."*

I want to grow old like a redwood tree,
producing harder wood each day, and more of it.

I want to live to the age of 1500
rooted, and rooting, in Northern California.

I want my biography to be titled
The Picture of Dorian Redwood.

The story opens with the discovery of a portrait,
a painting of a wrinkled weeping willow,
hidden high in my canopy. After several centuries
of satisfying sexual adventures, the story ends
as I'm felled by a jealous logger
who suffers from erectile dysfunction.

Shooting Chauvet: The World's Oldest Cave Art
 — *National Geographic*, January, 2015

The Voices at Chauvet Cave

After seeing Werner Herzog's "The Cave of Forgotten Dreams"

We are artists who know nothing
of art criticism, who didn't need you
to discover us or evaluate our work.

Like all artists, we create because we must.

This is not a museum or a temple.
It is simply a cave where we choose
to honor the animals who feed and clothe us,
and the great ones fast enough to elude our spears.

These are not abstractions.
The animals with eight legs run fast,
the ones with twelve run faster.
Those are the great ones we will never taste.

These are the stories of our hunt.
We hunt for food and clothing,
and we honor our kill.

Most of all we do not draw for you.
We do not seek your praise, or your speculation.
We do not know you, could not have imagined you.

If we had known, we would have prayed
for a tighter seal when the cliff face fell
over the entrance to our cave.

Kennedy Pledges Man on the Moon
  — BBC News, May 25, 1961

Telescope

I learned about the moon from my Uncle Norman. Uncle Norman had a telescope and we had a night sky undimmed by city lights. It was a match made in the heavens. And it was a time when America still cared about real science. We reeled at Russia's progress, launched an Echo to chase after Sputnik's head start. And as it gave chase, newspapers published Echo's orbit schedule, which Dad cut out and taped on the kitchen wall. We'd watch it pass over once or twice each night and occasionally spot the second, slightly dimmer Sputnik, and we'd shudder in the cold war.

On his visits, while the August sky darkened, Uncle Norman would play the piano, and we'd sing some of the old tunes: "It's Only a Paper Moon," "Shine on Harvest Moon;" we'd go sailing along "On Moonlight Bay." Then we'd head out the back door to the perfect platform for his telescope, the concrete slab that covered our cistern. We'd douse ourselves with mosquito repellent, set up the lawn chairs, and put out the porch light. Then, as we waited for the Perseid meteors to pierce the sky, we learned about the moon. Why it waxes and wanes, why the full moon rises at sunset, how it causes the tides, what created the craters that define its face. *No one has ever seen the other side of the moon!* he'd say. And in 1960, that was a true statement. Those were days of hope and inspiration. We were going to the moon! Maybe exploring space would finally unite the human race.

Instead, we planted our own partisan pennant there. We beat the Russians, and the Cold War continued. And even when the Cold War ended, other wars, real wars, raged on. The days of inspiration and real science are fading memories as Strategic Air Command and Space Force missile defense systems shield the moon's serenity.

O Metzli, O Bahloo, Mama Quilla!
O Igaluk, Hanwi, Máni!
O Diana and Artemis!
Our failed species admits
we don't deserve you.

'Coronavirus baby boom'? It's likely as
America braces for condom shortage
— *Miami Herald*, March 19, 2020

Pan-Demonic

Bacchus would be proud of him.
Pan, the rutting horny goat god,
has outdone himself this time.

This one is better than the April Fool's
Day Blizzard of 1997. Better than the
New York City Blackout of 1965.

Bigger than Woodstock!
Bigger than Mardi Gras
and Rio's Carnival combined.

The Celtic peoples had their Beltane,
the Germanic tribes their Walpurgis,
and the Romans their Floralia.

But ever since the Catholic Church
succeeded in turning those ancient
Spring fertility festivals into religious

holy days of penance and observance,
Pan has been plotting his revenge.
He'd be damned if he'd stand by

and let processions of crucifixes
and candles replace young maidens
dancing around a Maypole.

His pièce de résistance, the coup de grâce,
would be forced hibernation, a Pan-demic!
A cancellation of national sporting events

so no distractions would sublimate natural
animal springtime lusts. And best
of all, church services canceled! Afraid

to venture out for condoms, and not
knowing when the covert virus might come
knocking on their bedroom doors, humans

give in to their natural urges. People
party like the end is near,
which it surely is.

Screw abstinence!
Screw Lenten penances!
Screw Easter's solemnity!
Just Screw!
Praise Pan!

The Pope appoints the first woman deputy secretary
with the right to vote in the Synod of Bishops
— verietyinfo.com, February 7, 2021

Two Millennia of Misogyny

I gave up on the Catholic Church
in 1970. Their attitude toward women
was a contributing factor.

Sister Nathalie Becquart's appointment
as a voting member the Synod
is being ballyhooed as a great step forward
by the men of the established patriarchy.

This too-little-too-late news makes me glad
that I didn't string along for five decades
waiting for the church to see the light.

Misogyny and pedophilia, pillars
of the church. I'm not anti-Jesus.
Jesus was a revolutionary.

He loved Mary Magdalene
and left us no evidence
of a preference for young boys.

Universe Crueler, More Uncaring Place Than Previously Thought
— *The Onion*, July 3, 2013

Universe

after Richard Brautigan

Since 2013, I have searched in vain
for a poem that responds to this headline.

I have sat quietly for hours waiting
for it to come to me. I've arrived at the conclusion

that it's never going to arrive. Which
I guess, I kind of expected.

9
Obituaries

Every day the news is a script like a cement truck of neoliberal terror already in progress.

Rejected ideals party bosses don't share. A violent thunderstorm can invade. It's never going to arrive.

We will be there in our thousands. He's not breathing, he's begging, and the gumption it might take to change things.

What is one life worth? Just hours before the earth shook. And now women are flying again, driven by junkyard vultures, gold, platinum, and palladium. they sang just for us.

Poetry will be shouted from rooftops and railway stops, days of hope and inspiration, just the stitching in the patchwork.

Innocent by anyone's standard, your red, white, and blue heart. It doesn't shine for you and these few words: austerity, crisis, foreclosure.

There's only one amendment.

We create because we must.

Shirley Temple Dead: Legendary Child Star Dies at 85
 — *Hollywood Reporter*, February 11, 2014

On the Good Ship Lollipop

Let no alcohol be poured today.
Shirley Temple is dead at eighty-five.

Let us raise eponymous sweet concoctions
of fruit and bubbles and toast Clark Gable,
whose Hollywood star was eclipsed
by a six-year-old supernova
who earned 1,250 dollars a week
during the Depression.

In her honor, let all those with long locks
wear exactly fifty-six curls, her trademark, today.

Let us strap on tap shoes, don sailor suits,
and dance once more with Mr. Bojangles.

Let us all become ambassadors to foreign lands

Shirley Temple is dead at almost eighty-six.
The Good Ship Lollipop has sailed the River Styx.

World Shocked by US Execution of Troy Davis
— CNN, September 22, 2011

We All Lay Down

I'm not saying Troy Davis is innocent.
Troy Davis said it. Some witnesses said
he was guilty, then recanted.
Said they were coerced by police.
I'm not saying Troy Davis is innocent.
I'm saying there's doubt.
I'm saying murder is murder,
especially state-sanctioned killing.
I'm saying lynching is still legal in Georgia;
ropes, no longer around necks,
strap men to gurneys, hold them there
for four hours while learned judges deliberate.
No mercy.

I'm not saying Troy Davis is innocent.
I'm saying you could have been Troy Davis.
Or me. Given other circumstances,
Clarence Thomas or Barack Obama
could have been Troy Davis.

I'm not saying Troy Davis is innocent.
I'm saying the state of Georgia is guilty.
I'm saying America is guilty.
I'm saying we're all guilty.

We all lay down on the gurney
and took the needle.

Baseball legend Hank Aaron, who began and ended his big-league career in Milwaukee, dies at 86
— *Milwaukee Journal-Sentinel*, January 22, 2021

His Hammer

For 23 years, like a carpenter
he brought his tools
and a working class ethic
to the workplace.

Jackie had broken down the door
in 1947 and begun the deconstruction
of that old white edifice
that barred people of color.

Hank walked in Jackie's footsteps
letting his tools do the talking.
His bat, carried quietly like Teddy's big stick,
hammered out 40 homers year after year.

As he approached the Babe's record
small-minded resentful racists
were ruthless in their hatred
threatening him and his family.

The closer he came to Ruth,
the more vile their threats became
in the hopes he'd give up
and their white idol would be safe.

But Hammerin' Hank was a craftsman
who showed up for work every day.

He chiseled his own epitaph
into the granite stone
of the baseball record book.

Alex Trebek, Longtime Host of 'Jeopardy', Dies at 80
 — *New York Times*, January 7, 2021

My Main Man Alex

Game show host to the intelligent
and the autistic.

How many times I've chanted
five minutes to Jeopardy!

like Dustin Hoffman's
Rain Man character, Ray.

Sometimes I wonder
to which group I belong more.

We are all on the spectrum
somewhere.

Lawrence Ferlinghetti, Poet Who Nurtured the Beats, Dies at 101
  —*New York Times*, February 23, 2021

The Smiling Mortician Foiled

After nearly 102 years you finally tired
of waiting for the American Eagle
to drop those arrows from its talons
and join the parliament of birds
in their search for a rebirth of wonder.

Yes, after nearly 102 years of waiting
for a disarmed eagle, its wings clipped
to address an avian summit, confess
and repent, you gave up, you stopped
for death and waited patiently

while it caught up with you, panting.
Then, just as that smiling mortician
was catching its breath, just as
it raised its scythe for the harvest,
I saw Elijah's fiery winged chariot

swoop down with the gulls,
swing low and gather you,
the last of the great prophets
and carry you away, blazing
and still breathing.

You are not imagining it: We're all having
intense corona virus dreams
   — *Los Angeles Times*, April 7, 2020

Cicadas

"No one told them the world had ended." –Mark Doty

It was cicadas he was talking about.
No one had told them we were gone,
as if they sang just for us.

I dreamed of an earth a million years ago.
Maybe it was a million years from now.

In any case, there were cicadas
and the cicadas were singing.

Acknowledgements

I wish to thank the following periodicals and anthologies that first published the listed poems, some in slightly different versions.

Blue Collar Review: "Droning On," "Dying for Capitalism," "Horror Film," "Mine," "Plutocracy," and "Teaching Women How to Fly"

Brackish Zine: "Coping Strategies"

Brawler Lit: "Transportation Blues"

Camel Saloon: "Still Life"

Love at the Villa Nelle: "Second Thoughts"

Mobius, the Journal of Social Change: "Do Not Stare Directly"

New Verse News: "Another Useless Headline Poem," "Austerity," "If Only," and "Not Who We Are"

Spitball: "Ernie"

Tawdry Bawdry: "The Picture of Dorian Redwood"

Verse Virtual: "Pan-Demonic"

Verse & Vision: "The Voices of Chauvet Cave"

Verse Wisconsin: "We All Lay Down"

Bramble Lit: "Karleton and Robert"

Jerry Jazz Musician: "Minute Sonnet"

Lunch Bucket Brigade: "His Hammer," "The Empire Drones On," and "The Smiling Mortician"

Poetry Hall: "Facts and Anti-Facts"

So. Florida Poetry Journal: "Cicadas"

Verse-Virtual: "Gawker"

Special Thanks

I'd like to thank the Hartford Avenue Poets for their on-going support and encouragement. Many of these poems were greatly improved through our workshop meetings. And my poetry has continued to improve over the years with the valuable assistance of our critique group.

Much gratitude as well to Margaret Rozga, David Southward, and Dan Denton for their generous comments found on the back cover.

Thanks to Kathryn Harrington for her careful proofreading of the advance copy.

I'd like to thank Signe Jorgenson, signejorgenson.com, for her invaluable assistance with this manuscript. I highly recommend her work.

Finally, thanks to Dawn Hogue at Water's Edge Press for her faith in this book.

Ed Werstein, Milwaukee, Wisconsin, is a regional VP of the Wisconsin Fellowship of Poets. He is a sustaining member of *Blue Collar Review*. His poems have appeared in over 50 different journals and anthologies. Werstein's poetry has been nominated for a Pushcart Prize. In 2018 he received the Council of Wisconsin Writers Lorine Niedecker award. His book, *A Tar Pit To Dye In*, is available from Kelsay Books.

Follow the Author

edwerstein.com

www.ingramcontent.com/pod-product-compliance
Lightning Source LLC
Chambersburg PA
CBHW022012120526
44592CB00034B/791